Aphrodite: The Origins and History of the Greek Goddess

By Andrew Scott & Charles River Editors

The Birth of Venus by Botticelli

About Charles River Editors

Charles River Editors is a boutique digital publishing company, specializing in bringing history back to life with educational and engaging books on a wide range of topics. Keep up to date with our new and free offerings with this 5 second sign up on our weekly mailing list, and visit Our Kindle Author Page to see other recently published Kindle titles.

We make these books for you and always want to know our readers' opinions, so we encourage you to leave reviews and look forward to publishing new and exciting titles each week.

Introduction

An ancient statue depicting Aphrodite

Aphrodite

"However impious the apotheosis of sexuality may seem in the light of the Christian tradition, modern sensibility can nevertheless also appreciate how in the experience of love the loved one and indeed the whole world appears transfigured and joyously intensified, making all else seem insignificant, a tremendous power is revealed, a great duty."[1]

Attempting to cover all the forms the "Goddess of Love" encapsulates is no small affair. The roles she played in romance, marriage, procreation, and all of the other desires of humanity were myriad, but the aim of this book is to paint a slightly different, perhaps more esoteric version of Aphrodite from the usual image of her in mythology books.

---

[1] Burkert 1996

The fact is that Aphrodite, as an ancient Greek goddess, was not the anthropomorphic personage modern aficionados see painted on canvas and hewn out of stone. In addition to that, she was also so much more, which can be a difficult concept for the modern reader to discern. In fact, it was difficult for certain ancient readers to discern too; the 5th century BCE philosopher Plato expressed disgust at the idea that his gods would debase themselves in the adulterous, murderous, and mischievous ways they were said to have in their myths. However, it is important to remember that Plato represented a very small proportion of ancient Athenian society, and the rest of the populace didn't seem to have much of a problem including the "personal" anthropomorphic aspect of the gods into their more "elemental" and "essential" beings. As the scholar Leopold Schmidt put it, "For anyone born a Greek and thinking like a Greek, the idea of a clean antithesis between unity and plurality is put aside where the supernatural beings are concerned. He has no difficult in conceiving unity of action divorced from any unity of person."[2]

This is a very important point to remember when considering any of the ancient Greek gods, which can help the modern reader realize the depth of "character" that Aphrodite embodied for the ancient Greeks. Hers was more than the wooing gifts, more than the marriage bed, and more than the "propriety of women". She was an elemental force and not one to be underestimated.

Aphrodite: The Origins and History of the Greek Goddess of Love looks at the story of the legendary deity and the various roles she played in Greek mythology. Along with pictures depicting important people, places, and events, you will learn about Aphrodite like never before.

---

[2] Schmidt 1882

The Origins of Greek Mythology

"The Titanomachy symbolizes the victory of Order over Chaos." - Niall Livingstone[3]

"the Greek word Mythos can indicate, amongst other things, a public utterance expressing the authority of its speaker."[4] In fact, by the Classical Period, myths were principally instructive, hence Plato's dim view of these stories being in the hands of anyone but philosophers. Myths helped crystallize beliefs and fashion a means of observing and categorizing patterns in daily life. According to Hesiod, the "Pre-World" was populated by personifications;[5] he painted the picture of the primordial geography of his worldview by dramatizing the personification of those elements he considered primal. This is a perfectly arbitrary folkloric trope, but in the case of the ancient Greeks, the antagonism was infused with strains of uncomfortable duality. Hesiod's intention was to glorify Zeus, but in doing so, he created a melodrama that would last the ages.

[3] 2011
[4] Livingstone 2011
[5] Dowden 2011

Marie-Lan Nguyen's picture of a bust of Plato

The "Chasm" mentioned by Hesiod is a synonym for the ancient Greek word for Chaos, and "Earth" is the mighty mother-goddess Gaia, in whom was located the hellish Tartara (or Tartarus), where the Titans would ultimately meet their fate. Interestingly, Hesiod also places Eros, the embodiment of erotic love, at the conception of the cosmos too, thus providing the ancient Greek readers with a foundation for procreation and the lasciviousness of all deities. As a result, the act of creation begins with Chaos, Gaia (Mother Earth), and Eros (Erotic love), but these are no quaint grandparental figures or benign personifications. Chaos was capable of "giving birth" to the most macabre, inherently bleak, and "chaotic" elements of the world, without the need for a reproductive partner.

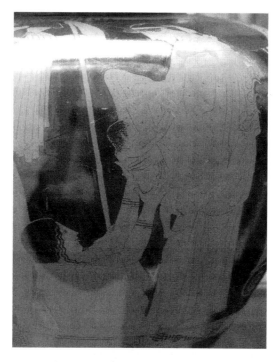

An ancient Greek depiction of Gaia handing her newborn, Erichthonius, to Athena as Hephaestus watches

Chaos spontaneously "bore" both Erebus (Darkness) and Nyx (Night), whose offspring were suitably morbid and must be credited as such in order to lessen the blame on Pandora for "bringing all the sorrow into the world." The list of Nyx's offspring reads like a dreaded guest list of the worst attributes of humanity: the Fates, Death Spirits, Nemesis (Retribution), Apate (Deceit), Geras (Old Age), Eris (Strife), Ponus (Toil), Lethe (Forgetfulness), Limus (Famine), the Algaia (Sorrows), the Hysminae (Fights), the Machae (Battles), the Phonoi (Murders), the Androctasiae (Manslaughters), the Neicea (Quarrels), Pseudea Logoi (Lies) the Amphillogiae (Disputes), Dysnomia (Lawlessness), Ate (Delusion), and finally, as a frail light in the darkness and the law that maintains it, Philotes (Friendship), and Horcus (Oath). It's important to remember these bleak personifications are the inhabitants of the world into which the Titans would be born. From the very beginning of Hesiod's *Theogony*, the reader is greeted with an array of reasons as to why "order" is to be honored and achieved at any cost.

Seeing that Chaos had no need for her, Gaia had to become her own catalyst for the cosmos.

Gaia "bore" Ouranos (Sky), whom Hesiod refers to as "Starry Heaven," so that "he should cover her all about, to be a secure seat for ever for the blessed gods." It wouldn't be long, however, before said "Starry Heaven" had lost all connection with any "security" for the gods or otherwise.

Gaia's incestuous union with her firstborn son would become the most decisive act in the early stages of the Greek cosmological story, but it also set the scene for the discernible world in which the ancient Greeks lived, with a fertile Earth embraced by an all-encompassing Sky. Out of this visible union were born the "insatiably bellicose"[6] Hecatoncheires (the "Hundred-Handed Giants"), the Gigantes (the Giants), as well as the famous one-eyed Cyclopes, who were credited with building those very same "great walls of the palace of Mycenae." The most powerful, first generation beings, whose monstrous power would become pivotal to the war that was to come between the gods and the Titans, are credited with laying the bricks and mortar of this mystical prior power structure. This connection between a real human past and the deeds of the divine is indicative of Hesiod's idea of a "Golden Age," in which humans and divine beings inhabited the same plane of existence and candidly interacted with each other. As this makes clear, even after two centuries of no significant building works, the crumbling walls of ancient palaces still had the power to awe and inspire theories of a divine past.

[6] Vernant 1996a

Johann Heinrich Wilhelm Tischbein's depiction of Polyphemus

Unlike the first generation of Ouranos and Gaia's offspring–not to mention those who simply materialized out of Chaos–the Titans had more ambiguous roles in early mythology. As Kerényi noted, "these titans are a mysterious group; to suggest that they were originally nature-gods is almost meaningless, and the truth is that we have no idea where most of them come from."[7] Unlike their forebears, Hesiod gives the Titans very few ostensibly "personified" names but instead gives them more rounded personalities. Here, the reader can begin to see a progression from chaos to order with every succession of power:

Bedded with Heaven (Ouranos), Gaia bore deep-swirling Oceanus, Koios and Kreios and Hyperion and Iapetos, Thea and Rhea and Themis and Mnemosyne (Memory), Phoebe of gold diadem, and lovely Tethys. After them the youngest was born, crooked schemer Chronos, most fearsome of children, who loathed his lusty father.[8] This is Hesiod's first account of the names of the first 12 Titans. "Deep-swirling Oceanus" refers to the enormous river the Greeks believed encircled their world. Mnemosyne, the Titan of "Memory," would go on to sleep with her nephew, Zeus, and give birth to the famous Muses, those favorites of the poets who inspired Hesiod to write his account. Aside from these two Titans, the names are not personifications, but individualistic. Rather than represent any ubiquitous force or element, their own characters and actions take hold of the story, and the reader is ushered into a new epoch of protagonists and antagonists, especially when it comes to that "crooked schemer," Chronos.

---

[7] 1963
[8] *Theogony Lines 133-138*

A Roman mosaic depicting Ouranos and Gaia

Hesiod refers to the Titans as "chthonic." They were "born of the Earth," and their subsequent "imprisonment" within her defines them even further. Ouranos hated his children, and once born, he forced Gaia to place them back inside her and guard them there indefinitely. Ouranos had no intention of curbing his lust for Gaia–no doubt caused by his primordial uncle Eros–and he "enveloped" her even while she was pregnant, though he would not allow "nature" to come to pass afterward. It's here, in Hesiod's *Theogony*, that the reader gets the first glimpse of an aberration of nature, with a wicked father overpowering a divine mother.

To Ouranos, all those that were born of Earth and Heaven were the most fearsome of children, and their own father loathed them from the beginning. As soon as each of them was born, he hid them all away in a cavern of Earth, and would not let them into the light. He took pleasure in the wicked work, while the huge Earth was tight-pressed inside, and groaned. Finally, she thought up a nasty trick. Without delay, she created the element of grey adamant, made a great reaping hook, and showed it to her dear children and spoke to give them courage, sore at heart as she was: "Children of mine and of an evil father, I wonder whether you would like to do as I say? We could get redress for your father's cruelty. After all, he began it by his ugly behaviour."[9]

This appeal to the Titans to avenge the injustices brought upon them by their wicked father would be echoed by their own offspring, and the "call to arms" would come to symbolize the transition of one power system to another, according to a "natural law of behavior" (since it was the ugliness of Ouranos's behavior that would lead to his downfall). Here, the reader is faced with another common mythological trope: that of creating a tool for one purpose, only to have it used by another, somewhat contradictory purpose later on.

In order to usurp their wicked father, Chronos would use a new element specifically created for the purpose: Adamant. This element would become the metal of choice for the weapons the gods would later wield in their revolt against their own wicked father, the original "adamant-wielder," Chronos. The demise of Ouranos would not only liberate Gaia and the Titans, but would also result in the creation of yet more players in this primordial divine theater.

After Gaia handed Chronos the adamant sickle and explained to him the "stratagem," the defining moment of separation took place: "Great Heaven came, bringing on the night and, desirous of love, he spread himself over Earth, stretched out in every direction. His son reached out from the ambush with his left hand…with his right he took the huge sickle with its long row of sharp teeth and quickly cut off his father's genitals, and flung them behind him to fly where they might."[10]

The Sky was cleaved from Mother Earth, and both she and the Titans were liberated from tyranny. From the conservatively described "drops of blood" were born the Giants "in gleaming armour with long spears in their hands," the nymphs who would occupy the woods and forests of the world and the Erinyes, the so-called "Furies" who would hunt down and punish those perpetrators of the most heinous crimes known to humankind. After he cut off their genitals, Chronos threw them into the sea, where they floated in a "white foam." Out of this foam–or "Aphros" in ancient Greek–sprang forth the first goddess. Just as Eros had been present at the establishment of the first power system, Aphrodite, the more elaborate representative of love and desire, would be present to usher in the next.

---

[9] *Theogony Lines 159-161*
[10] *Lines 170-187*

Sandro Boticelli's painting of the birth of Aphrodite

Peter Paul Rubens" picture of Chronos devouring one of his children

Liberated from their manumission and in the presence of Aphrodite, there came a new surge in reproduction amongst the Titans. A plethora of new deities, rivers, nymphs, and monsters appeared and assumed their roles in the new cosmos, governed by the sons and daughters of that wicked Ouranos. As mentioned earlier, their offspring wasn't inherently wicked, as they included such beings as Helios (the Sun), the Horae (the Seasons), and thousands of wood and sea nymphs. This is worth bearing in mind when considering the role of the Titans as antagonists later on.

After a lengthy description of the unions of the Titans and the fruit they bore, Hesiod turns to the moment where Rhea, "surrendering to (her brother) Chronos, bore resplendent children:" "Hestia, Demeter, and gold-sandaled Hera, mighty Hades who lives under the earth, merciless of heart, and [Poseidon,] the booming Shaker of Earth, and Zeus the resourceful, father of gods and men, under whose thunder the broad earth is shaken."[11]

In typical fashion, Chronos learned from Gaia and Ouranos that it was fated for him to be defeated by his own child (Hesiod doesn't explain when his castrated father gave him this proclamation). Having learned something from his father–namely that Gaia couldn't be trusted to imprison her offspring and they would eventually have to be set free upon the world–Chronos decided to devour his children as they were born. In her suffering, Rhea appealed to her parents–Gaia and Ouranos–for a stratagem to save her children from this fate. Gaia told her to go to a town called Lyktos in Crete to give birth. When she did, Gaia accepted the youngest god, Zeus, into a mountain on that fateful island and wrapped a stone in "babycloth" to give to his voracious father in lieu of the child. Chronos swallowed the stone without so much as a sneaking suspicion he was about to be overthrown, like his father had been before him.

[11] *Lines 454-460*

An illustration depicting Rhea giving the stone to Chronos

Chronos regurgitated each god in reverse order, the stone coming first and falling at Delphi, where it was venerated thenceforth. With this "re-birth" of the gods, the scene was set for a cataclysmic confrontation and an apocalyptic power struggle. Vengeance had to be exacted for the rape of their mother and their own imprisonment. The first twelve Titans had given birth to most of the ubiquitous elements of the cosmos. Not only did this create the backdrop for a new order of rule, but it was also the fertile ground from which all stories–mythological and factual–could grow and be imbued with meaning, according to the cosmological order.

The "titanomachy"–the war wreaked upon the Titans–was a defining moment in the evolution of Greek mythological thought. It was the moment where the Greeks developed a "greater self-awareness of their own social life and thought"[12] in the face of the "barbaric other," and it was so

---

[12] 1984

much more than a fight of "good versus evil," as is often thought to be the case.

The term "titanomachy" is a compound word, incorporating "titan" and the Greek word "Machia," meaning "fight" or "battle." Just like the Amazonomachy (battle against the fearsome Amazons) and the Centauromachy (battle against the Centaurs), the Titanomachy was depicted in the metopes of the Parthenon in Athens. The scenes selected for the metopes were those depicting quintessential "battles against the other." The Parthenon was a monument erected in the wake of the Persian Wars, the biggest, most cataclysmic invasion the Greeks had suffered in 700 years. Although this was a fight against "the other," it was a defining moment in ancient Greek history and of the mind-set of that peculiar collective. Their relatively young power systems had faced seemingly insurmountable odds against an older kingdom and had survived victorious, quashing chaos and constructing order from the rubble.

Cornelis Cornelisz van Haarlem's "The Fall of the Titans"

Joachim Wtewael's "The Battle Between the Gods and the Titans"

A depiction of Zeus launching a thunderbolt on the Temple of Artemis at Corfu

Although the epic poets Homer and Hesiod "attributed to the divine powers everything that is harmful and blameworthy in men: stealing, committing adultery and deceiving one another,"[13] the Titans were depicted as something worse, embodying the rule of disorder and hubris. Although the gods were fallible and innately "human" in their vices, they were ultimately progressive. The Titans were "chthonic," representing "Nature" in the battle against the more "cultured"–and certainly, more elaborate–personalities of the Olympian gods, who in this episode, are representative of order and culture.

Ultimately, the Titanomachy is a classic story of the revolt[14] of the new against the old, culture against nature, and order against chaos. It is a story indicative of a people who have undergone multiple power struggles and states of unrest. As is the case with most cultures, the ancient Greeks defined their contemporary state of existence by the series of "boundary catastrophes" that had preceded it.[15] For that reason, the Titanomachy wasn't just another piece of "art as propaganda," but instead a defining moment in ancient Greek culture.

The Myths of Aphrodite

There are three different myths of Aphrodite's birth. One of those myths paints her as a daughter of Zeus, whom he sired with the oracular goddess Dione. Dione's oracle was at the great city of Dodona and was, most likely, the oldest oracle in Greece. Aphrodite was, in fact, often referred to as "Dione" in certain later texts. There is a theory that this could have been because the word "dione" is actually the "genitive" form of "dios", meaning "god" or "Zeus". This would suggest that Aphrodite belonged to Zeus, making her little more than "one of his many other children".

The most famous of the myths of Aphrodite's birth, however, gives her primacy over all of the gods and the titans. Gaia, the Earth Mother, bore herself a husband called Uranos, but he turned out to be a lecherous beast who covered Gaia every night and forced himself upon her. From this union came a litany of children: the Titans, the 'Hundred-Handed Ones', and the single-eyed Cyclopes. Uranos hated his children, and once they were born, he forced them deep inside their mother again until she groaned with the strain of bearing their weight. One day, anticipating her husband's nightly arrival, she called to her children within her and asked who would wield the glorious sickle she had secretly fashioned to finally rid her of her burden. Not the Cyclopes, or Hundred-Handed Ones, or any of the oldest Titans came to her aid except for Chronos. The youngest Titan told his mother that he would emancipate her, and she handed him the sickle and told him to lie in wait for his wicked father's return. Chronos did so, hidden beneath the earth, and when his father covered Gaia once again, he leapt from his hiding place and attacked. He

---

[13] Vernant 1983
[14] Detienne 1981
[15] Breton Connelly 2014

succeeded with his first blow, castrating his father. Blood flowed from the wound onto the earth, and from the drops rose the dreaded Erinnyes, feared mistresses of vengeance, and also the fearsome Giants and the nymphs of the ash tree, whose roots would bear the most bellicose and warlike creatures and arms on Earth. Chronos took the severed genitals and threw them into the sea, and suddenly foam began to form around them. They floated and created a foam that tipped the crests of the waves, until they arrived at Crete, and floating on a scallop shell, Aphrodite emerged from the foam and stepped foot on the shore.

The legendary birthplace of Aphrodite

The third myth, however, takes place long before Chronos or Uranos. In the earliest days of the cosmos, there was nothing but Chaos. No darkness nor light, no land nor sea existed except that eldritch void out of which all had to be born from itself. Out of the Chaos came Gaia and hellish Tartarus and then Night and Day. Oceanus emerged and spread itself across the earth, and then, out of the same hopeless void, Aphrodite appeared, dancing across the waves. Some say that Eros was born to Chaos as well, and he and Aphrodite became companions as she danced across the surf. First she danced to the island of Cythera, but she saw this was too meagre, too simple an island for her to make her home, so she continued to travel across ocean and land, and grass and flowers erupted from the earth wherever she laid her feet. She travelled to the Peloponnese and then to Paphos on Cyprus, which she claimed as her home and where she was worshipped henceforth.

Aphrodite and Eros brought love and passion to the cosmos, and thanks to them, the Titans and the Gods came together and populated the world. Seeing that she was without a husband, however, Zeus betrothed her to the lame smith god Hephaestus, who fell in love with her deeply at first sight of her loveliness. But laughter-loving Aphrodite found Hephaestus repugnant, and she turned her gaze to the other gods in search of a more fitting mate. The authority of Zeus and his brothers, Hades and Poseidon, held no attraction for her, and even the youthful beauty of Hermes and Apollo couldn't strike a fire in her heart. Instead, it was Ares, the formidable god of war, who caused her to cuckold poor Hephaestus, as Odysseus heard at his feast with the Phaeacians: "The minstrel struck the chords in prelude to his sweet lay and sang of the love of Ares and Aphrodite of the fair crown, how first they lay together in the house of Hephaestus secretly; and Ares gave her many gifts, and shamed the bed of the lord Hephaestus."[16]

Ares and Aphrodite seized the moments when Hephaestus was away from home. Yet they were cautious too. Not wanting to be found out by any of the gods, Ares brought young Alectryon to guard the chamber door and watch for the ascension of Helios, the sun, who saw all that his light touched. He told Alectryon to wait for the first light to hit the horizon and then call out to the clandestine lovers and warn them of Helios's approaching gaze, lest the sun tell Hephaestus of his wife's infidelity.

On one such night, Ares and Aphrodite made love beneath the covering of Hephaestus's bed and continued well into the morning, undisturbed by warnings from the youth outside. Alectryon had fallen asleep before Helios ascended, and when the light landed on the lovers' bed, the sun god sped to Hephaestus to tell him what he had seen. "And when Hephaestus heard the grievous tale, he went his way to his smithy, pondering evil in the deep of his heart, and set on the anvil block the great anvil and forged bonds which might not be broken or loosed, that the lovers might bide fast where they were. But when he had fashioned the snare in his wrath against Ares, he went to his chamber where lay his bed, and everywhere round about the bed-posts he spread the bonds, and many too were hung from above, from the roof-beams, fine as spiders' webs, so that no one even of the blessed gods could see them, so exceeding craftily were they fashioned."[17]

Later that night, Hephaestus strung the gossamer chain net from bedpost to bedpost, stretching invisibly beneath the awning. The smith god told his wife he was going to visit his most beloved people on the island of Lemnos, and he departed without a hint of his ken. Aphrodite waited until her husband was out of sight, and then she called to Ares, who had been awaiting the all clear. Ares brought her gifts and whispered sweet words in her ear until she agreed to leave her

[16] Homer Odyssey 8.265-280
[17] ibid.

sumptuous royal hall for the comforts of her marital bed. They were naked before they reached the bed, and once they fell upon it in their embrace, the delicate chain fell from the awning and trapped them, unmoving in the position in which they fell. When the sun rose again, Hephaestus heard of his bittersweet success and called to his father, Zeus, to bring all the gods and goddesses to the chamber where the prisoners lay and look upon his wife's shame and that of Ares, now bound hopelessly together.

All the gods came from Mt. Olympus and made the land tremble with their laughter at the guilty pair. But the goddesses abstained, either out of propriety or disgust, and never saw Aphrodite's and Ares's shame. Hephaestus told Zeus that he wanted him to return the betrothal gifts he had given him before his wedding to Aphrodite, but Zeus said he would pay nothing to a fool who would make public his wife's infidelity and left the palace. Meanwhile, the other gods looked on at heavenly Aphrodite's beauty and whispered to each other. "To Hermes the lord Apollo, son of Zeus, said: 'Hermes, son of Zeus, messenger, giver of good things, wouldst thou in sooth be willing, even though ensnared with strong bonds, to lie on a couch by the side of golden Aphrodite?' Then the messenger, Argeiphontes, answered him: 'Would that this might befall, lord Apollo, thou archer god thrice as many bonds inextricable might clasp me about and ye gods, aye, and all the goddesses too might be looking on, but that I might sleep by the side of golden Aphrodite.'"[18]

Then Poseidon, who had fallen in love with Aphrodite on first sight of her naked body, told Hephaestus that Ares should have to pay a fine for his actions that was equal to the price the smith god paid in wedding gifts. Hephaestus agreed and implored Zeus to enforce the punishment. Zeus told Hephaestus that he was a fool for bringing the affair to the attention of the rest of the gods, and that there was no way he would enforce such a punishment on Ares. Poseidon sympathized with Hephaestus and told him that, if Ares did not pay his fine, Poseidon would pay the fine and marry Aphrodite himself.

At this, Hephaestus lifted the chain, and the lovers fled the palace in shame. Ares, after cursing Alectryon to become a cockerel and always alert the people to the rising sun, fled to Thrace, the land of his birth. Aphrodite disappeared to Cyprus and bathed in the sea to renew her virginity. Thus, it was Ares's children, not Hephaestus's children, that Aphrodite first bore and handed to the unfortunate smith god. She bore him dreaded Phobos ("Fear") and Deimos ("Terror"), who later drew Ares's chariot in war, as well as the inescapable goddess of revolt and just retribution, Adrestia. But she also bore him the much sought-after Harmonia, who so often followed in her father's wake, and the blessed Erotes, gods of love and sexual intercourse, who made up Aphrodite's retinue from then on.

With her virginity renewed and her shame subsided, Aphrodite visited Poseidon. Although she didn't offer him her hand in marriage, she did spend the night with him as she was flattered by

---

[18] Iliad 8.334-342

his kind words. She also spent the night with Hermes for the flattering comments he made while she was entangled, and to the two gods she bore three children: Rhodus and Herophilus to Poseidon and the double-gendered Hermaphroditus to Hermes. In the end, Hephaestus couldn't extinguish his love so easily, and he took her back, infidelity and all.

Though she was, perhaps, one of the oldest deities in the Olympian Pantheon, Aphrodite was still exceedingly quick to take offense, as King Cinyras of Cyprus soon found out. King Cinyras had a daughter called Smyrna, whose beauty was famed across the island and beyond. Her parents were so proud of their daughter's beauty that they were apt to boast of it to their friends and acquaintances, but Cinyras's wife took her pride too far when she boasted that Smyrna's beauty could equal that of the goddess of love herself.

When Aphrodite heard about this slander, she decided to repay it by making Smyrna fall passionately in love with her own father. One night not long after, Smyrna managed to convince the nurse to make her father too drunk to take note of his actions, and she climbed into bed with him for the night. The next morning, Cinyras realized what had happened, and he chased Smyrna from the palace, waving a sword at her and threatening to murder her in his wrath. He chased Smyrna across his kingdom, but when he caught up to her on a hill and was about to murder his own daughter, Aphrodite felt bad for the innocent girl and changed her into a myrrh tree in the nick of time. Cinyras's sword had already been unleashed, however, and it came crashing through the tree, splitting it in two and revealing a beautiful baby boy within.

Aphrodite swept the child away and hid him in a chest, which she brought to Persephone in the Underworld and asked to hide it in a dark place until she came back to claim it. Shortly after Aphrodite left, however, Persephone grew curious and opened the chest. She was immediately enchanted by the beauty of the young child she found inside.

Years later, Aphrodite heard that the Queen of the Dead had brought the child up in her palace and had subsequently taken him as her lover. She flew down to the Underworld and demanded Persephone return him to her. Persephone refused. Aphrodite appealed to Zeus to settle the dispute, but once again, Zeus chose to take no part in settling the affairs of love and lust and delegated it to the Muse Calliope instead. Calliope decided that both women had just claims to Adonis, since Aphrodite was the cause of both his birth and salvation and Persephone had brought him up in her palace. She then declared that Adonis should spend a third of the year with each and have a third of the year to do with as he pleased.

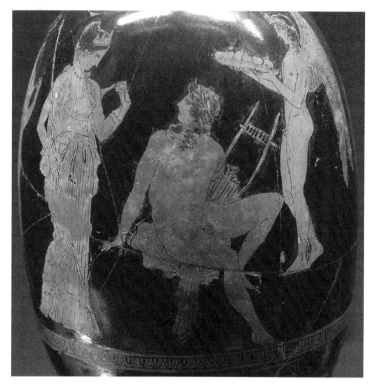

A 5ᵗʰ century BCE depiction of Aphrodite and Adonis

However, Aphrodite did not play fair by the accord they struck. The goddess of love donned her magic girdle that inspired love in any who saw it, and she tempted Persephone's lover into not only spending his own third of the year with her, but also begrudging the third he was required to spend with Persephone too. Persephone was furious with Aphrodite, and so she traveled to Thrace and told Ares that his lover now preferred Adonis, a mere and effeminate mortal, to him.[19] Ares was seized with jealousy, and when he saw Adonis hunting on Mount Lebanon, he took on the form of a boar and gored him to death. When Aphrodite arrived to find her lover bleeding to death on the mountainside, she saw that the first Anemones had sprouted from the red pools of his blood, and these came to be associated with the young lover henceforth. Aphrodite was distraught and pleaded with Zeus to make an arrangement with Persephone so that Adonis would spend no more than half the year in the land of the dead. Zeus agreed, and Adonis was one of the few mortals to be granted a reprieve from an eternity among the dead.[20]

[19] Graves 1966

The Death of Adonis **by Luca Giordano**

Though she is the goddess of love, Aphrodite's part in bringing about the Trojan War cannot be overstated, and it was at the wedding of Thetis and Peleus where the dreaded die was cast. After he learned that their progeny would likely cause his demise, Poseidon stopped pursuing the beautiful sea nymph Thetis and arranged for her to be married to the aged king of Thessaly. All the gods were invited to the sumptuous feast and glorious wedding Poseidon arranged for his former paramour. All, that is, except Ares's sister Eris.

Eris, or "Strife", was furious with this slight, and she immediately began orchestrating her revenge. She took one of the famous golden apples from the garden of the Hesperides and carved upon it the simple message 'To The Fairest'. Then, unseen by the reveling gods, she sneaked down to the wedding and dropped the apple in such a way that it rolled into the space between Hera, Athena, and Aphrodite.

The goddesses read the inscription and, not questioning where the apple came from, each presumed without doubt that it was addressed to her. Naturally, the other two had something to say about this presumption, and soon Zeus was asked to mediate the decision of who was the fairest between them. Zeus was not one to adjudicate a decision between his wife and anybody, so he passed that duty on to a young Trojan herdsman named Paris.

---

[20] ibid.

Paris arrived at the wedding and told Zeus that he simply could not decide between them. Then the goddesses started to offer gifts. Hera offered the young herdsman rule over all of Europe and Asia; Athena offered him wisdom and strength in battle; but Aphrodite, who was made even lovelier with the help of the Graces and Seasons, approached Paris naked and offered him the hand of the most beautiful woman in the world. Paris had heard of Helen of Sparta's beauty, and though she was married to the warlike Menelaus, he immediately consented to awarding Aphrodite the apple. "Discord" was brought to the Mediterranean.

10 years later, the world was still feeling the effects of Aphrodite's actions and Menelaus's response. The Greeks and Trojans had been well matched, and the Greeks just could not bring down the magnificent walls of Troy. Then Agamemnon's insult to Achilles tipped the balance in favour of the Trojans, and the gods found themselves embroiled in the mire too.

Hera and Athena, still furious at Paris's decision, chose to side with the Greeks, whereas Aphrodite sided with Paris's countrymen. When Achilles, furious with Agamemnon for appropriating what he saw as his rightful spoils of war, refused to fight, Paris called to Menelaus and offered a duel to settle the war once and for all. Menelaus, who was 'loved by Ares', was a much better fighter than Paris and soon stood over the former herdsman, ready to land the killing blow. Aphrodite could not bear to watch one of her favorites die, however, so she spirited Paris away before the blow could land.

When they saw this divine outrage, the Greek army engaged the Trojans, and yet another battle ensued. Aphrodite remained on the battlefield to protect her son, the Trojan Aeneas, from certain death at the hands of Diomedes. Cut short in his murderous rampage, Diomedes was furious with Aphrodite, and abandoning all pious propriety, he chased the goddess down. "He the while had gone in pursuit of Cypris with his pitiless bronze, discerning that she was a weakling goddess, and not one of those that lord it in the battle of warriors, no Athene she, nor Enyo, sacker of cities. But when he had come upon her as he pursued her through the great throng, then the son of great-souled Tydeus thrust with his sharp spear and leapt upon her, and wounded the surface of her delicate hand, and forthwith through the ambrosial raiment that the Graces themselves had wrought for her the spear pierced the flesh upon the wrist above the palm and forth flowed the immortal blood of the goddess, the ichor, such as floweth in the blessed gods; for they eat not bread neither drink flaming wine, wherefore they are bloodless, and are called immortals. She then with a loud cry let fall her son, and Phoebus Apollo took him in his arms and saved him in a dark cloud, lest any of the Danaans with swift horses might hurl a spear of bronze into his breast and take away his life. But over her shouted aloud Diomedes good at the war-cry: 'Keep thee away, daughter of Zeus, from war and fighting. Sufficeth it not that thou beguilest weakling women? But if into battle thou wilt enter, verily methinks thou shalt shudder at the name thereof, if thou hearest it even from afar.'"*21* Aphrodite fled the battlefield and arrived, bleeding ichor at

---

21 Iliad 5.330-351

Zeus's side on Mount Olympus. Zeus chided her for doing anything other than her duty — that of setting human hearts ablaze.

The war raged on, with gods and mortals striking blows for their allotted sides, until Zeus grew furious with the gods' meddling and forbade them from taking any more part in the human conflict. All the gods bore this decree uncomfortably as they watched their sons and favorites fall to the sword, so Hera turned to her former adversary for help in the name of the greater good as she saw it. Hera planned to enchant her husband with her beauty, and while he slept, the gods would be free to disobey Zeus's orders and take part once again in the war. "'It may not be that I should say thee nay, nor were it seemly; for thou sleepest in the arms of mightiest Zeus.' She spake, and loosed from her bosom the broidered [girdle], curiously-wrought, wherein are fashioned all manner of allurements; therein is love, therein desire, therein dalliance— beguilement that steals the wits even of the wise. This she laid in her hands, and spake, and addressed her: 'Take now and lay in thy bosom this [girdle], curiously-wrought, wherein all things are fashioned; I tell thee thou shalt not return with that unaccomplished, whatsoever in thy heart thou desirest.'"[22]

Hera succeeded in bewitching Zeus with her charms and Aphrodite's girdle, and the gods' plan was successful, though only one side eventually emerged victorious. Zeus, for his part, was furious with both his wife and with Aphrodite, for though such actions ought to be expected of the goddess of love, this was not the first time that Aphrodite had bewitched him with her magic girdle, and this irked Zeus to his core.

Aphrodite's girdle was as beautiful as its wearer, and it was said to embody the unrelenting force of love itself. The gods often asked Aphrodite to borrow her girdle, or asked her to use it to inspire love in the merest of mortals they took their fancy to, and Aphrodite rarely refused them. The girdle made mortals frail to the charms of the gods, and simply seeing Aphrodite wearing it was often enough to ensnare immortal hearts to her as well. All except Zeus's, that is. He never slept with the goddess of love, but chose to live in constant temptation instead.

Aphrodite often laughed at the other gods for their desire for mortals, wondering what it could be that could attract them to imperfection, to fleeting prettiness that couldn't hold a candle to the beauty of the divine. One day, however, furious with Aphrodite's scorn for the gods' affairs and exhausted by his constant desire for her, Zeus sought his revenge. "Upon Aphrodite herself Zeus cast sweet desire to be joined in love with a mortal man, to the end that, very soon, not even she should be innocent of a mortal's love; lest laughter-loving Aphrodite should one day softly smile and say mockingly among all the gods that she had joined the gods in love with mortal women who bare sons of death to the deathless gods, and had mated the goddesses with mortal men.

---

[22] Iliad 14.211-221

And so he put in her heart sweet desire for Anchises, who at that time among the steep hills of many-fountained Ida was tending cattle, and in shape was like the immortal gods. Therefore, when laughter-loving Aphrodite saw him, she loved him, and desire seized her in her heart. She went to Cyprus, to Paphos, where her precinct is and where a fragrant altar was located, and passed into her sweet-smelling temple. There she went in and put to the glittering doors, and there the Graces bathed her with heavenly oil such as blooms upon the bodies of the eternal gods —oil divinely sweet, which she had by her, filled with fragrance. And laughter-loving Aphrodite put on all her rich clothes, and when she had decked herself with gold, she left sweet-smelling Cyprus and went in haste towards Troy, swiftly travelling high up among the clouds.

So she came to many-fountained Ida, the mother of wild creatures and went straight to the homestead across the mountains. After her came grey wolves, fawning on her, and grim-eyed lions, and bears, and fleet leopards, ravenous for deer: and she was glad in heart to see them, and put desire in their breasts, so that they all mated, two together, about the shadowy coombes."[23]

Aphrodite appeared to Anchises in his herdsman's hut in the form of a Phrygian princess. She appeared in a red cloak, and the king was so enchanted by her beauty that he lay with her that night, making love amongst the animal belts and beneath a cloud of softly buzzing bees. The next morning, Aphrodite put a spell on Anchises to ensure he slept while she transformed back into her natural state and prepared to reveal herself to him. She spoke to him, and he woke to find that he was in the presence of a goddess. Looming, she was huge and dazzled him with her divine brilliance. Anchises was a humble and pious king, and he knew the fate that usually befell mortals who had witnessed the naked body of a goddess. He dropped to his knees in the herdsman's hut and begged Aphrodite to spare his life. The goddess laughed at his worries, and she told him to rise. She said to him that their union would bring forth a strong son who would become famous for founding a great city. That son would be Aeneas, who would leave the burning city of Troy and travel across the seas to found Rome.

---

[23] Homeric Hymn to Aphrodite 54-72

William Blake Richmond's painting of Aphrodite and Anchises

Sadly, for all his piety, Anchises was not a subtle man, and his fate was sealed one night when he was drinking with his compatriots. Discussing the merits of various women in the city, one of his drinking mates asked the king if he wouldn't rather sleep with a particular girl than the goddess of love herself.[24] With no hint of irony, Anchises turned to the man and told him matter-of-factly that since he had already slept with both, the question was moot. Zeus heard this comment and took it as a slight against Aphrodite. He launched one of his thunderbolts fromMount Olympus, and it would have struck the king dead had it not been for Aphrodite, who threw her magic girdle in its path and deflected the bolt to the ground. However, the force of the bolt blasted Anchises across the room, and he was crippled for the rest of his days.

The Origins of Aphrodite

The origins of Aphrodite are vague and obscure, but they do highlight certain interesting consistencies in her character. Below, the 8th-7th century BCE poet Hesiod put in poetic form the etymology of her name in his description of her birth as a result of Chronos's castration. "And so soon as he had cut off the members with flint and cast them from the land into the surging sea, they were swept away over the main a long time: and a white foam spread around them from the immortal flesh, and in it there grew a maiden. First she drew near holy Cythera, and from there, afterwards, she came to sea-girt Cyprus, and came forth an awful and lovely goddess, and grass grew up about her beneath her shapely feet. Her gods and men call Aphrodite, and the foam-born goddess and rich-crowned Cytherea, because she grew amid the foam."[25]

---

[24] Graves 1966
[25] Theogony 189

"Aphros", meaning "foam", has come to be the accepted etymology for the first half of Aphrodite's name. The second part "-dite" has been equated with the suffix "-ditē", or "bright", which was a common epithet not just for Aphrodite, but also for many goddesses in the ancient Greek pantheon. Some scholars believe that the second half of Aphrodite's name comes from the suffix "-oditē" meaning "wanderer", which would lend itself to the other myth of Aphrodite's birth, in which she emerges out of Chaos and dances across the waves to Cythera and then "wanders" until she arrives in Cyprus. There are other suggested etymologies of her name, but since many of them refer to either Mycenaean or earlier languages, they are fraught with difficulty.

The Mycenaean Period (ca. 1600-1100 BCE) saw the advent of the first syllabic script of the earliest Greek language scholars have been able to translate. This script is known as Linear B, and references to many of the gods of the later Greek pantheon can be found in various forms within it. However, Aphrodite and her other forms cannot be found in this script, so any reference to her etymology as having Mycenaean elements simply cannot be corroborated to a sufficient degree of accuracy that would allow it to be accepted by most modern scholars.[26]

However, the earliest attestations of Aphrodite's name do indeed coincide with her attributes as a goddess of love. According to Liddell & Scott's Greek lexicon, the verb form "Aphrodisiazo" relates to both the act of sexual intercourse and also the act of "indulging in lust". This would suggest a relative consistency with her name and her later character from her earliest appearances in the Greek language.

Her consorts, Eros and Himeros, contribute etymologically to her character too. "Eros" was the old abstract noun for "love", and it appears as early as the 8th century BCE in the writings of both Hesiod and Homer. "Himeros" can boast an equally early attestation as the abstract noun for "yearning", particularly the uncontrollable yearning brought on by love.

It is a curious case to have three "birth" myths for any deity in Greek mythology, and there is no shortage of irony in the fact that evidence of contradicting desires can be seen in the differences of these myths. No extreme mental exertion need be employed to see the hand of the ancient Greek patriarchy in giving Aphrodite a father in the form of Zeus. Without this parentage, Aphrodite appears unwieldy, an elemental force who represents an image of "woman" that didn't fit within the ancient Greek idea of what a daughter, wife, and mother should be — that is, liberated.

This "foreignness" was not just a patriarchal projection, however. The ancient Greeks often referred to Aphrodite, as they did to Dionysus, as a "foreign" deity that was brought into Greek culture at an "earlier date". The historian Herodotus, who wrote about his curiosity for non-Greek cultures at length — even if he didn't actually manage to travel to these places himself —

---

[26] Burkert 1996

makes this foreignness of Aphrodite explicit in his *Histories*. When discussing the march of the Scythians through Syria towards Egypt, Herodotus relates the following tale. "From there they marched against Egypt: and when they were in the part of Syria called Palestine, Psammetichus king of Egypt met them and persuaded them with gifts and prayers to come no further. So they turned back, and when they came on their way to the city of Ascalon in Syria, most of the Scythians passed by and did no harm, but a few remained behind and plundered the temple of Heavenly Aphrodite. This temple, I discover from making inquiry, is the oldest of all the temples of the goddess, for the temple in Cyprus was founded from it, as the Cyprians themselves say; and the temple on Cythera was founded by Phoenicians from this same land of Syria."[27]

The idea that Aphrodite was originally an Eastern goddess appropriated by the ancient Greeks at the onset of their great cultural revolutions of the Archaic Period (ca. 8th century BCE) is one that has been corroborated by modern and ancient historians alike. Here Herodotus can be of some help again. "As to the customs of the Persians, I know them to be these. It is not their custom to make and set up statues and temples and altars, but those who do such things they think foolish, because, I suppose, they have never believed the gods to be like men, as the Greeks do; but they call the whole circuit of heaven Zeus, and to him they sacrifice on the highest peaks of the mountains; they sacrifice also to the sun and moon and earth and fire and water and winds. From the beginning, these are the only gods to whom they have ever sacrificed; they learned later to sacrifice to the 'heavenly' Aphrodite from the Assyrians and Arabians. She is called by the Assyrians Mylitta, by the Arabians Alilat, by the Persians Mitra."[28]

Here the name "Zeus" would have obviously been a translated name, equivocal to Herodotus's consideration of the "head" of the Greek pantheon in the 5th century BCE, at the time of his writing. However, the order of worship in this context is similar to the Greek understanding of Aphrodite's birth, particularly the myth that has her appear out of chaos, dancing on the waves to her 'native' Cyprus. Herodotus gives her different names according to the place of her worship, but most scholars today believe that ancient Greek worship of her is most closely tied to the ancient Phoenician goddess of love Ishtar-Astarte.

Again this ties in with Herodotus's claims that the "oldest temple" to Aphrodite was in Syria, the home of the Phoenicians, and the character of Ishtar-Astarte corroborates this claim further. Ishtar-Astarte was not only the Phoenician goddess of love, but she was also the "Queen of Heaven". To the Greeks, who often "translated" foreign gods directly into their own pantheon according to their characteristics, this would make Astarte-Ishtar "Aphrodite Ourania", or "Heavenly", who was that same Aphrodite considered to have been older than the gods. This celestial version of Aphrodite was more elemental than the later version of her as a simple goddess of amorous liaisons. She was a goddess who, just as the sky covers the earth, embodied the inevitable force that influenced all creatures beneath her. Curiously, to the Phoenicians, this

[27] Herodotus 1.105
[28] Herodotus 1.131

goddess was also androgynous, which would later be a key element to the character of Aphrodite.

The connection between Astarte-Ishtar and Aphrodite goes even further. Aside from sharing the same "Heavenly" name, both goddesses were worshipped with incense altars and sacrifices of doves, something that was unique to Aphrodite in ancient Greek religion.[29] Astarte-Ishtar was a warrior goddess too, and Aphrodite, when depicted wearing armor, was also believed to bestow victory upon those she favored. The final similarity, it seems, between the two goddesses is their part in prostitution. Astarte-Ishtar was the goddess of the "Hetaerae", whom historians today usually define as "companions" or "courtesans" and are distinguished from the more mundane "Pornai" by the fact that the Hetaerae were well educated and they often reserved their services for a select and smaller group of clients, with whom they had longer-term relationships. Some scholars believe that Aphrodite was also a patroness of the Hetaerae, further building upon the evidence of a direct connection between her and the Phoenician Astarte-Ishtar.

There is yet another interesting aspect to the earliest myth of Aphrodite's birth. The "Foam-Wanderer" was said to have danced first to Cythera and then to the Peloponnese before finally making her home on Cyprus. This appears to represent an important trade route held by the Minoan Empire. The Minoan Empire stretched from northern Greece to Egypt and incorporated many of the islands and coastal cities from the Mediterranean between ca 3000 and 1100 BCE. Some historians believe that it was partly the work of the Minoans, along with the Phoenicians, that Aphrodite was translated to the Greek civilization. The Cretan version of the goddess was very closely associated with the sea, and the floor of her palace sanctuary at the Minoan capital at Knossos is festooned with shells. Archaeological excavations have unearthed a gem of this goddess blowing on a Triton shell and none other than her tragic lover's symbol, a sea anemone, set beside her altar. It seems that these two objects were especially sacred to this Aphrodite-esque goddess since many of these objects, or terracotta replicas, were found in late Minoan tombs.[30]

Thematically, Aphrodite's birth also betrays her Near-Eastern origins. Mythologist G. S. Kirk takes the "Structuralist" approach to the study of myths, meaning he finds the key themes that occur in myths from different cultures and extrapolates meaning from them. By being born of the male-inseminated sea, Aphrodite embodies the classic Indo-European mytheme of "unusual births" that are replicated from the Mediterranean to India. She is the product of a violent castration, but unlike the King Erichthonius, who was born from Hephaestus's semen inseminating the land of Athens, Aphrodite belongs to the sea, and hers is the foam of the waves, the shore, and the denouement of her father's rule.

---

[29] Burkert 1996
[30] Graves 1955

Worship of Aphrodite

"So saying the mighty Hephaestus loosed the bonds and the two, when they were freed from that bond so strong, sprang up straightway. And Ares departed to Thrace, but she, the laughter-loving Aphrodite, went to Cyprus, to Paphos, where is her demesne and fragrant altar. There the Graces bathed her and anointed her with immortal oil, such as gleams upon the gods that are forever. And they clothed her in lovely raiment, a wonder to behold. This song the famous minstrel sang; and Odysseus was glad at heart as he listened."[31] This passage comes from Homer's *The Odyssey*, when Odysseus feasts with the Phaeacians and listens to the shameless exploits of Aphrodite and Ares in Hephaestus's bed. Although this is certainly a literary invention much later than the original worship of Aphrodite in Greek religion, there is one aspect of the bard's story that is much older: Aphrodite's home being on Paphos in Cyprus.[32]

"The Cypriote" is the most commonly used epithet for Aphrodite from the works of Homer onwards, but there is evidence to suggest that she may have been considered as such from as early as the 9th century BCE.[33] When the Phoenicians first left their capital of Tyre to start colonizing in the 9th century BCE, there was already a Mycenaean temple at the site of Paphos. However, since there is no evidence of Aphrodite in the Mycenaean texts, the temple's conversion by the Phoenicians at this time can be seen as the origin of the story of her residence there, especially considering the Mycenaean temple was originally converted to a temple of Ashtar-Istarte.[34]

Another famous temple to this goddess, and later to Aphrodite, is found at the site of Amathus, also on Cyprus. Here archaeologists have discovered an "Eteo-Cypriot" script and language that, despite having been in constant use from this time down to the Hellenistic Period (323-31 BCE), is yet to be deciphered. It is here that many votive offerings of naked women with hideous bird heads have been found and whose origins remain unknown. It is important to remember, however, that Cyprus's geographical location lent itself towards taking influences from many different cultures and civilizations, so this may be simply a result of artistic influence felt by the worshippers of the time. However, until the Eteo-Cypriot script is deciphered, the meaning behind this theriocephaly will continue to be a mystery.

There is some evidence of larger, less personal cults of Aphrodite that are also in keeping with her Phoenician heritage, in particular the cult of Aphrodite Euploia. The name "Euploia" is a compound epithet made up of the words "eu", meaning "well", and "ploia", meaning "voyage". Naturally, this demonstrates Aphrodite's connection with the sea, but worship of her in this form had a very specific focus. The cult of Aphrodite Euploia had as its center a temple in the Athenian port of Piraeus, and it was here that sailors implored the goddess to "make the sea

---

[31] Homer's Odyssey 8.363
[32] Kirk 1996
[33] Burkert 1996
[34] ibid.

smile as she did".[35] This temple was not as grand as the temple of Poseidon on nearby Sounion, who was known to cause earthquakes and storms, but the two gods actually played slightly different roles in the case of the sea. Although both were powerful and easily offended, Poseidon was apt to cause storms at sea, and sailors would worship him in order to appease and thus avoid his wrath. Poseidon's whims sank ships. Aphrodite Euploia, on the other hand, was propitiated by the sailors to use her charms to appease Poseidon's wrath, and therefore hers was the role of a protector rather than a volatile force who needed to be assuaged.

Her role as a "benevolent protector" may come as a surprise to anybody who is familiar with the story of Hippolytus and Aphrodite. At the beginning of Euripedes's play, which is the most famous telling of this myth, Aphrodite appears to be anything but the benevolent protector of the Piraeus. "Mighty and of high renown, among mortals and in heaven alike, I am called the goddess Aphrodite. Of all those who dwell between the Euxine Sea and the Pillars of Atlas and look on the light of the sun, I honour those who reverence my power, but I lay low all those who think proud thoughts against me. For in the gods as well one finds this trait: they enjoy receiving honour from mortals."[36]

Here Aphrodite sounds more like the disgruntled goddess who attacked Smyrna (before regretting her actions and saving the princess's son), and she is depicted as such for the rest of the play. There is no "laughter-loving" or "smiling" Aphrodite in the story of Hippolytus, whom she punishes for choosing a life of celibacy and hunting over worshipping love. However, the literary and archaeological evidence from Athens suggests that the ancient Greeks in general saw Aphrodite in a much more benevolent light than one might presume from Euripedes's play.

The epithet "Pandemos" is another compound name made up of "pan", meaning "all", and "demos", meaning "people". In this respect, Aphrodite is seen as "for everybody" in Athens. To the Western reader, the idea of a deity whose worship is not accessible to all society may come as a surprise, but this was certainly the case in ancient Greece; the pantheon of gods each had his or her own epithets that effectively constituted a separate role and, in some cases, a distinct change in character. Depending on the epithet, Apollo was either the god of medicine or the "rainer down of plagues". Furthermore, there were aspects of religious society that were forbidden to residents of a city for various reasons, such as their gender, age, and whether they held citizenship or not. An excellent example of this would be the Athenian festival the "Thesmophoria". Held in honor of Demeter and her daughter Persephone, the Thesmophoria was a fertility festival with restricted access to just adult female citizens.

There is very little literary evidence that helps the modern reader understand just what is meant by Aphrodite's epithet "Pandemos". However, it is true that in Plato's *Symposium*, he distinguished between two types of "Aphrodite" in the following way. "What sort [of

---

[35] Parker 2007
[36] Eur. Hippolytus 1-5

Aphrodite/Love] we ought to praise. Now this defect I will endeavour to amend, and will first decide on a Love who deserves our praise, and then will praise it in terms worthy of its godhead. We are all aware that there is no Aphrodite or Love-passion without a Love. True, if that goddess were one, then Love would be one: but since there are two of her, there must needs be two Loves also. Does anyone doubt that she is double? Surely there is the elder, of no mother born, but daughter of Heaven, whence we name her Heavenly; while the younger was the child of Zeus and Dione, and her we call [Pandemos]."

Here Plato defines the second type of love, Pandemos, as something that is "common" or "base", a thing for animals rather than that intellectual "high" love to which his name later became attached. This is entirely unsurprising in as much as it was typical "Platonic" sophistry, but outside of the Symposion, the term 'Pandemos' can still be interpreted in two ways.

In his excellent work, *Polytheism and Society at Athens*, historian Robert Parker highlights the two possible interpretations for Aphrodite "Pandemos". The first, he says, could be that "Pandemos" simply refers to the fact that Aphrodite is accessible to all inhabitants of Athens, regardless of the defining characteristics that may prohibit someone from worshipping her. The second is that "Aphrodite was also seen as a power who by her gentle charms creates friendship and concord among the citizens."[37]

In this case, Aphrodite's cult may have been seen as a cult of civic unity. Parker goes on to make an important point about one of Aphrodite's children, Peitho. Peitho, meaning "persuasion", represented both political rhetoric and erotic 'allure'.[38] Furthermore, Peitho was given a civic sacrifice every year by the inhabitants of Athens, which probably took place in the very temple of his mother as "Pandemos". Until more literary or archaeological evidence surfaces to prove one theory over the other, however, Aphrodite's role as a civic goddess will remain almost as obscure as her origins. What is clearer, though, and what should be much less surprising, is the importance of her role as a "personal" rather than a "civic" goddess.

Evidence of the "personal" in the historical record is often reserved for persons of civic importance. Therefore, outside of war, politics, and great works of art and architecture, the average citizen's voice remains largely unheard. Thanks to individual votive offerings uncovered at various sanctuaries, however, historians are able to discern the echoes of individuals, and nowhere are those echoes more felt than in the worship of love. The study of the location of temples, in particular, has revealed some interesting facts about ancient Greek worship. Giving a temple "pride of place" on an acropolis would, undoubtedly, betray a city's allegiance to one god or goddess fairly ostensibly, but the choice of location can be more nuanced than that.

---

[37] 1996
[38] ibid.

The precipitous slopes of the Athenian acropolis look like no fit place for honoring the gods, but the fact is that there are a surprising number of temples in and on those slopes, some of which appear to be clinging on for survival. However, as Robert Parker points out, this place of apparent neglect can actually embody the character and role of the deity perfectly. Take, for instance, the role of Pan. Pan was integrated into the ancient Greek pantheon much later than many of the other gods, and his pastoral nature did not align itself easily with dedicating a well-crafted temple to him. So, the ancient Athenian was left with the conundrum of wanting to honor the god according to his nature, while also incorporating his worship into the most sacred space in the city. This was achieved not through innovative architectural design that would encapsulate his character in hewn stone, but by simply placing Pan's centre of worship in a cave on the northern slope of the acropolis.[39]

In the case of Aphrodite, a similar preservation of nature and space took place on the slopes of the acropolis. She, along with Asclepius (the god of medicine) and Nymphe ("bride") all occupied temples clinging to the craggy slopes as "periacropolitan" gods. However, these gods did not occupy these sites because they were deemed less important to the average worshipper, but instead the very nature of their worship necessitated intimacy more than civic attention. Religion in ancient Greece was often a very public affair, and historians know that because there are copious records of festivals, processions, and civic sacrifices performed by priests who occupied very politicized roles. However, historians also know that to define ancient Greek religion as an entirely public matter would be rash and inaccurate. There is evidence of many gods to whom private, individual rites were held that did not even include the smallest civic structure: the family. Initiations into Orphic cults, privately conducted rites to Pan and Dionysus, and of course, appeals to Aphrodite were commonplace in Athens, even if the more grandiose historical record doesn't trumpet their occurrence.

Historian Walter Burkert made mention of the poetry of Sappho as being the place where Aphrodite's worship "finds its most personal and most complete expression." Sappho was a 7th century BCE poet from Lesbos, about whom very little is actually known. Her poetry mostly survives in fragments, but she was known throughout the Greek world as one of the great lyric poets whose main theme was love. Many of her poems of love (requited and not) are addressed directly to "The Cypriot" herself, and they paint a picture of the life of "maidens" and Aphrodite that is at once beautiful and enlightening. In his seminal work, *Greek Religion*, Burkert unifies the themes of Sappho's poetry excellently. "The circle of maidens who are awaiting marriage is bathed in the aura of the goddess, [Aphrodite] with garlands of flowers, costly head-dresses, sweet fragrances, and soft couches. Aphrodite is summoned to the festival, to descend to her sacred grove where magical sleep reaches down from the trembling leabes, and to pour our nectar, mixed with festal joys, like wine … The [Ode to Aphrodite] describes how Aphrodite of the brightly coloured throne descends to earth on a bird-borne chariot from her father's golden

---

[39] ibid.

homel she hears the entreaty of hervotary, she will turn the heart of the loved one so that the love will be returned: love alone prevents life from being overtaken by cares and weariness."[40]

Since Aphrodite was a goddess of allure and attraction, it may come as no surprise that Aphrodite's more "personal" worship also came from unmarried or recently married young girls. Ordinarily Aphrodite did not play much of a role in the religion of marriage and subsequent childbirth; that realm was very much left to Hera, Hestia, and Athena. However, in the case of the "Genetyllides", Aphrodite did play a part. The Genetyllides were spirits, or "Daimones", related to "birth" and were considered part of Aphrodite's retinue. In fact, the name Genetyllides is simply a diminutive for 'birth'. As part of her retinue, the Genetyllides were worshipped as "mediators" between the goddess of love and the act of childbirth. In this way, Aphrodite often appears as a goddess on the fringes of marriage as opposed to a central character as many modern readers would consider her to be today.

Newlywed girls and more mature wives would visit her sacred spring on Hymettus in order to be blessed with pregnancy and easy labor, and there they dedicated votive offerings in the form of breasts so as to ensure successful lactation and the rearing of healthy babies. Here Aphrodite's role as a goddess of the woman's body is very apparent. Aphrodite was the recipient of many similar votive offerings at her sanctuary at Daphni. Here archaeologists have discovered many offerings in the shape of breasts and female genitalia. Many historians today believe that such forms served two purposes for Aphrodite in her "fringe" roles. The first is that of facilitating pregnancy, childbirth, and lactation. However, since this is more often found to be the role of other, more "marital" goddesses, these offerings are considered to serve a propitiatory role for a goddess who was a "specialist" in women's health. At Daphni and Athens, Aphrodite and Artemis adopted this role in a sense "outside" the normal sphere of marriage.[41]

Parker says that most historians today suppose that Aphrodite's role in childbirth and marriage is, ultimately, the one that ensures "gaiety" in every aspect. The idea that Aphrodite was simply a representation of carnal lust is the product of much later representations of her. In fact, the representation of Aphrodite as nude and sensual in art lost favor amongst Greek artists in the 7th century BCE and only gained popularity again during the Roman period.[42] In the meantime, she was always represented with the finest clothing, and she was most commonly associated with necklaces and long, brightly colored robes such as the one in which she appeared to Anchises. In the second *Homeric Hymn to Aphrodite*, written at some point in the 7th century BCE, the work formulates the contemporary image of Aphrodite eloquently. "I will sing of stately Aphrodite, gold-crowned and beautiful, whose dominion is the walled cities of all sea-set Cyprus. There the moist breath of the western wind wafted her over the waves of the loud-moaning sea in soft foam, and there the gold-filleted Hours welcomed her joyously. They clothed her with heavenly

---

[40] 1996
[41] Parker 2007
[42] Burkert 1996

garments: on her head they put a fine, well-wrought crown of gold, and in her pierced ears they hung ornaments of orichalc and precious gold, and adorned her with golden necklaces over her soft neck and snow-white breasts, jewels which the gold-filleted Hours wear themselves whenever they go to their father's house to join the lovely dances of the gods."[43]

Although, as Parker puts it, the spheres of marriage and childbirth were "alien" to her, Aphrodite does indeed "intrude" on this sphere, and she appears with no diminishment to her character. When she appears, she represents a level of divine femininity that goes beyond what was seen as a respectable woman's duty in ancient Greece. She glorifies womanhood in her blessings and protection of the female body.

Aphrodite's Character

To define the character of a god, just as a person, one must look to both nature and nurture. In this sense, Aphrodite's origins and deeds are paramount to understanding the character that was built up over the centuries. However, since the presence of women is a taciturn one in history (to say the least), the modern historian must winnow out the prejudices of male writers and seek out the fundamental elements of Aphrodite's character wherever possible.

Aristophanes's play *Lysistrata* opens with the kind of telling view of society that only comedy can capture so perfectly. The play centers on Lysistrata and her group of fellow Athenian women, who are tired of the Peloponnesian War and see withholding sex from their husbands as the best way of forcing them to make an accord with their enemy, Sparta. Eventually, most of the female characters are presented as conscientious, anti-war activists; however, this comes at a steep price: resisting the power of their "base urges" long enough to make their husbands feel the pain of abstinence. Consider the opening dialogue of the play:

LYSISTRATA
If they were trysting for a Bacchanal,
A feast of Pan or Colias or Genetyllis,
The tambourines would block the rowdy streets,
But now there's not a woman to be seen
Except—ah, yes—this neighbour of mine yonder.
[Enter CALONICE.]

Good day Calonice.

CALONICE
Good day Lysistrata.
But what has vexed you so? Tell me, child.

---

[43] 1-15

What are these black looks for? It doesn't suit you
To knit your eyebrows up glumly like that.

LYSISTRATA
Calonice, it's more than I can bear,
I am hot all over with blushes for our sex.
Men say we're slippery rogues—

CALONICE
And aren't they right?

To a male audience, this kind of stereotype, contrasted with Lysistrata's activism, would have fit the prejudices of the day exactly. Women were considered more subject to their base emotions, and their religious activities, from which men were often forbidden, were suspected to be wild, orgiastic affairs in which they threw off the shackles of the patriarchal society. Perhaps indeed they were, but sadly, there aren't any prime sources written by the participants to help modern readers understand these events better.

With that in mind, it's possible to understand how a little-known story of Aphrodite and the Fates may have been perceived. By the time of Homer's writings, most of the gods' and goddesses' personalities were more or less fixed in the mythological canon.[44] Their nature in the subsequent stories changed little over the centuries, but on closer inspection, some of those myths reveal interesting characteristics. It was the Fates who allocated the various roles and duties to each of the gods and goddesses of Mt. Olympus. Aphrodite was given just one duty, that of making love, and when she was seen by Athena at a loom, the goddess of wisdom lost her head. Athena threatened to abandon all her duties if Aphrodite infringed upon her work as patroness of the loom ever again. Aphrodite apologized and, so it was said, never took up the loom again. This could have been seen as a comical anecdote at Aphrodite's expense, but when seen in the writings of Hesiod and in light of her Near Eastern past, Aphrodite's single role turns out to be quite the large one indeed.

As Burkert put it, "although it is ignored in the heroic epics, the birth myth is not a marginal extravagance of poetic fancy".[45] He refers to the myth of Aphrodite being born out of Chaos. Here Aphrodite is placed at the beginning of the cosmos, before all life. What does this mean, then, for the role of the goddess of love so early on? With Eros dancing upon the waves at her side, Aphrodite would appear to be the catalyst of all life in the universe. Without love, or at least lust and desire, the idea of procreation would have been unthinkable to the ancient reader, so placing her in this context would have made complete sense and would have been a dominating aspect of her character.

---

[44] Kirk 1996
[45] 1996

Take, for example, the myth of her affair with Anchises on Mount Ida. In the Homeric Hymn to Aphrodite, the author describes her arrival on Mt. Ida in terms of her calming the most violent beasts. Rather than being fearful of these savage creatures, as might be expected of a 'mere' goddess of love, Aphrodite delights in their company, turning to each and instilling within their hearts the inevitable force of passion. They paired off two by two in her wake, forgot their nature, and obeyed "the higher law of sexual union".[46]

Burkert also refers to Hesiod's myth of Aphrodite being born from Chronos's severed genitals, and he goes on to say that a familiar epithet of Aphrodite was actually as much the result of linguistic mutation as cultural perception. The common Homeric epithet for Aphrodite was "Laughter-loving" or, in the ancient Greek, "Philommeides". However, Hesiod gives her another, slightly different epithet: "Philommedes", meaning "to her belong male genitals".

Of course, her night with Hermes produced the double-sexed child Hermaphroditus, but Hesiod's epithet for Aphrodite seems to refer to a much earlier aspect of her character to which one must return to the Near East to explain. Aphrodite's prior incarnation, Ishtar-Astarte, was actually a dual goddess-god. Archaeologists have discovered images of Ishtar and Astarte sitting next to each other with the goddess Ishtar shown having a beard. There is also evidence of a much later Greek image of Aphrodite sitting next to an "Aphroditos" and also sporting a beard. Considering that love affects both men and women, it can hardly be surprising that these images exist. Aphrodite inspires men, women, and beasts to "obey their higher nature", so to her "belong" the genitalia of all, and this has been the way since the dawn of the cosmos. While she was most certainly a goddess whose duty pertained very much to women, the affairs of the heart are undiscerning of gender. Love is not a duty or a role; it is the "higher nature" that is the driving force behind the cosmos, whether for procreation or not.

Aphrodite and Death

"But come, let us take our joy, couched together in love; for never yet hath desire so encompassed my soul—nay, not when at the first I snatched thee from lovely Lacedaemon and sailed with thee on my seafaring ships …"[47] The myths involving Anchises and Smyrna both show Aphrodite as a bringer of death. In fact, famous historian and poet Robert Graves refers to her as the "Death-in-Life" goddess. However, in ancient Greek, the most common name for "Death" was in fact masculine ("Thanatos"), not feminine, and although Hesiod described him as having a "heart of iron," and "an implacable soul of bronze", this was simply because he could not be avoided. There is no malice in Thanatos, but simply eternal inevitability, yet there is a connection between Thanatos and Love, pointed out by the renowned scholar Jean-Pierre Vernant, "where the warrior's fight to the death shares a hazy boundary with the attraction and sexual union of man and woman."[48]

---

[46] ibid.
[47] Homer's Iliad 3.442

In Hesiod's myth of Aphrodite's birth, she appears born out of Chaos to no mother or father. However, her own birth follows a litany of children born out of Night, the first three of which are all words for Death: Thanatos, Moros ("destiny"), and Black Ker ("death in a female aspect"). Aphrodite, Eros, and the embodiments of death are kin at the beginning of time, but Aphrodite is also given a retinue of other characters too. Night also bears Philotes ("loving tenderness") and Apate ("deceit"), who are henceforth part of Aphrodite's purview too. Hesiod's comments, though certainly a product of a mindset that stretches back millennia, are undoubtedly misogynistic since he says that Philotes and Apate belong to Aphrodite and all women. This point of view is hardly surprising; after all, it was Hesiod who first documented the myth of Pandora, she who unleashed all evil on the world. In fact, prior to the creation of "woman", humans did not know death. So, on the advent of woman's entrance into the world, Hesiod writes that deceitful words and death accompanied her too.[49]

There is more to Hesiod than simple misogyny can account for, of course. The language he utilizes, though unacceptable by modern standards, unites the worlds of death and love in quite interesting ways. Take the word "Damazō/Damnēmi", for instance. This translates as "subjugate/tame". The ancient Greeks would talk about "subjugating a wife to make her my own", but they would also use the same word for "subjugation" of an enemy in war. It appears many times in Homer's *The Iliad*, with soldiers rattling their arms and boasting how they're going to subjugate the unworthy soldiers that dare face them. But the master of Damazō, the "subjugator of subjugators", in Hesiod's *Theogony*, is Eros. As Vernant puts it, "It is Eros whom Hesiod celebrates as having the power of subjugating every god and every mortal. Eros' master, the yoke he imposes, is the sign of a kind of magic, thelxis. Eros is a sorcerer. When he takes possession of you, he snatches you away from your ordinary concerns, out of the horizon of your day-to-day life, to open up a new dimension of existence for you."[50]

This is Eros's true power. More than a "power", it is a "force", one that people cannot escape, and as the quote from Paris exemplifies, completely "envelopes" one. That's how the ancient Greeks referred to love, like it was "enveloping" or "surrounds your head and your thoughts like a cloud, that he surrounds you and hides you."[51] Inevitable and all encompassing of one's senses, Eros transports people to another reality, just like death.

Hesiod, knowingly or not, takes the analogous language even further. Using the same terms Homer uses on the battlefield, he wrote that love has the power of breaking or weakening the knees, and that the look of a woman can have the same effect as a javelin that spills forth "life-blood" onto the battlefield. All of these terms employ the same verbs, and even Sappho, who was known to use Homeric language, used them too. In one of her poems, she wrote that Penelope's

---

[48] 1992
[49] ibid.
[50] 1992
[51] ibid.

suitors' knees "are loosened under the charm of love," a Homeric turn of phrase that is more often used to describe the final fall of a felled soldier in battle.[52]

Love, then — and it is good to remember that, for the ancient Greek, the retinue of a god or goddess is an aspect of that deity, just as a limb or appendage would be part of a person — is Aphrodite's most obvious aspect and also her most terrible. The ancient Greeks referred to "Winged Eros" swooping down to claim those he saw as most beautiful in the exact same way they described "Winged Thanatos" who makes people "disappear". In the case of "stealing away" mortals for whatever reason, the language is particularly clear. As Emily Vermeule put it, for the ancient Greeks, "love and death were two aspects of the same power, as in the myth of Persephone or Helen of Troy."[53]

Aphrodite the Powerful

"Of these three Aphrodite cannot bend or ensnare the hearts. But of all others there is nothing among the blessed gods or among mortal men that has escaped Aphrodite. Even the heart of Zeus, who delights in thunder, is led astray by her; though he is greatest of all and has the lot of highest majesty, she beguiles even his wise heart whensoever she pleases, and mates him with mortal women."[54] These "three" who cannot be bent or ensnared by Aphrodite are Hestia, Artemis, and Athena, the three goddesses who swore to remain virgins for eternity in order to fulfill their divine roles. Only three deities, out of the entire cosmos, are able to resist the charms of Aphrodite, and those charms are described in the same terms as weapons by the ancient Greeks. Her abilities are her panoply against which nobody can defend themselves. As Vernant explained, "Nothing can withstand her, neither the beasts nor men nor gods. But the goddess's prerogative is not the brutal domination and physical coercion appropriate to the warrior deities. Her weapons, even more successful, are tenderness and charm. No creature in the heavens, on earth, or in the sea can escape the magic powers of the forces she mobilizes: Peithō (persuasion), Apatē (alluring charm), Philotēs (the bonds of love)."[55]

Such "weaponry" is not hinted at in the most famous myths involving Aphrodite. In her affair with Ares, she is described as a beautiful, but wily victim of her own passions. The same is true of the myth in which Zeus makes her fall in love with a mortal, and it is true of her later, guilt-tarnished love for Adonis. But these are just a few instances of her appearances in myth; to understand her true character, the modern reader must look wider and must broaden an understanding of the episodes in which Aphrodite plays a part. In some cases, the ancient Greeks made it quite easy to do so.

---

[52] Carson 2002
[53] 1979
[54] Homeric Hymn to Aphrodite 34-40
[55] 2006

On the great statue of Zeus that occupied the temple at Olympia, all the gods are actually present. The sculptor carved the 12 main gods on the base of the statue, all lined up in pairs, flanked by the sun and moon, of male and female deities. All the pairs, marriages mostly, were laid out in a beautiful array of powerful mates — Zeus with Hera, Poseidon with Amphritrite, and so on — until, in the middle of all these pairs, as if basking in the good work they had done, stood Aphrodite and Eros, the powerful ones, catalysts of all.

Through it all, it becomes clear that Aphrodite's place in the pantheon and the society of ancient Greece was much more grandiose and imposing than that of a simple allurer and adulterer. Most modern books on ancient Greek mythology limit her role to those two aspects and, at times, mention the embarrassing episode with Diomedes on the battlefield of Troy. The fact that she was seen as possibly being the catalyst of all creation not only adds to her character, but also paints a more beautiful image of universal creation than exists in most modern cultures today. If love, not "obligation", "necessity", or "fancy", was the driving force behind the religious idea of creation, then love becomes a powerfully divine act in and of itself. Creating the universe for no more reason than to receive worship is the act of a selfish god, whereas Aphrodite's role in the creation myth of the ancient Greeks was one of curiosity and generosity. Furthermore, since she was an androgynous goddess, the domain of love and seduction is not reserved for just one half of the sexes. Hers is as much a universal role, as it was a role in creating the universe.

Online Resources

Other books about ancient history by Charles River Editors

Other books about ancient Greece by Charles River Editors

Other books about Aphrodite on Amazon

Bibliography

Berens, E. M., (2007) Myths and Legends of Greece and Rome New York

Burkert, W., (1996) Greek Religion Blackwell Publishers

Carson, A., (2002) If Not, Winter; Fragments of Sappho Vintage Books

Evelyn-White. H.G., (1914) The Homeric Hymns and Homerica Cambridge, MA. Harvard University Press

Frazer. J.G., (1921) Apollodorus, The Library Cambridge, MA, Harvard University Press

Fowler. H. N., (1925) Plato Vol. 9 Cambridge, MA, Harvard University Press

Godley. A. D., (1920) Herodotus Histories Harvard University Press.

Graves, R., (1955) The Greek Myths Penguin

Hansen, W. F., (2004) Handbook of Greek Mythology Oxford University Press

Hughes, D., (2013) Human Sacrifice in Ancient Greece Routledge

Kirk, G. S., (1996) Myth: Its Meaning And Function In Ancient And Other Cultures University of California Press

Liddell, H.G., & Scott, R., (1940) Greek-English Lexicon Clarendon Press

Lindsay, J., ed. (1984) Complete Plays of Aristophanes Bantam Classics

Mallory. J.P and Adams. D.Q., (1997) Encyclopaedia of Indo-European Culture

Edited by J. P. Mallory, Douglas Q. Adams

Meyer. M. W., (1987) The Ancient Mysteries: A Sourcebook Harper Collins

Murray. A.T., (1924) Homer's Iliad Cambridge MA, Harvard University Press

Murray. A.T., (1919) Homer's Odyssey Cambridge MA, Harvard University Press

Ormerod. H.A. and Jones. W.H.S. (1918) Pausanias Description of Greece Cambridge MA, Harvard University Press

Orrieux, C. & Schmitt Pantel. P., (1995) A History of Ancient Greece Blackwell Publishing Ltd

Parker, R., (2007) Polytheism and Society in Athens Oxford University Press

Rieu, E.V., (1959) The Argonautica of Apollonius of Rhodes Penguin

Ruck. C.P and Staples. D., (2001) The World of Classical Myth: Gods and Goddesses, Heroines and Heroes Carolina Academic Press

Schmidt, L., (1882) Die Ethik der altern Griechen Hertz

Seaton, R. C., (1912) Apollonius Rhodius Argonautica Loeb Classical Library

Taylor, T., (1987) The Orphic Hymns Philosophical Research Society

Vermeule, E., (1979) Aspects of Death in Early Greek Art and Poetry Berkley

Vernant, J.P., (1992) Mortals and Immortals Princeton University Press

Vernant, J. P., (1996) Myth and Society in Ancient Greece Zone Books

Vernant, J. P., (2006) Myth and Thought in Ancient Greece Zone Books

Vernant, J. P., (1982) The Origins of Greek Thought Cornell University Press

Way, A.S., (1913) Quintus Smyrnaeus: The Fall of Troy Loeb Classical Library

Free Books by Charles River Editors

We have brand new titles available for free most days of the week. To see which of our titles are currently free, click on this link.

Discounted Books by Charles River Editors

We have titles at a discount price of just 99 cents everyday. To see which of our titles are currently 99 cents, click on this link.

Made in the USA
San Bernardino, CA
18 May 2018